Twelfth Night

WILLIAM SHAKESPEARE

● for Key Stage 3 ●

Guide written by

Ron Simpson

A *Letts* EXPLORE **Literature Guide**

First published 1999
Reprinted 2001, 2002

Letts Educational,
The Chiswick Centre,
414 Chiswick High Road,
London W4 5TF
Tel: 020 8996 3333

Series editor Jo Kemp

Typeset by Jordan Publishing Design

Text design Jordan Publishing Design

Cover and text illustrations Ivan Allen

Acknowledgements

British Library Cataloguing in Publication Data
A CIP record for this book is available from the British Library

ISBN 1 85758 863 0

Printed and bound in Great Britain

Ashford Colour Press, Gosport, Hampshire

Letts Educational Ltd, a division of Granada Learning Ltd. Part of the Granada Media Group.

■ Contents

TWELFTH NIGHT.

DUKE ORSINO IS LOVESICK FOR OLIVIA...

IF MUSIC BE THE FOOD OF LOVE, PLAY ON...

1

MEANWHILE, ON THE SEA COAST...

I'LL SERVE THIS DUKE.

2

VIOLA/CESARIO HAS A MISSION.

BE NOT DENIED ACCESS, STAND AT HER DOORS...

3

OLIVIA MOURNS FOR HER DEAD BROTHER.

I KNOW HIS SOUL IS IN HEAVEN.

4

I CANNOT LOVE HIM.

HE LEFT THIS RING...

SHE LOVES ME SURE.

ON THE COAST, ANOTHER SURVIVOR COMES ASHORE...

I AM BOUND TO ORSINO'S COURT...

ORSINO AND VIOLA ARE BOTH TROUBLED BY UNREQUITED LOVE.

TO HER IN HASTE. GIVE HER THIS JEWEL.

SHE NEVER TOLD HER LOVE.

OLIVIA'S STEWARD DREAMS OF MARRYING HIS MISTRESS...

..AND SOME HAVE GREATNESS THRUST UPON 'EM.

10

MORE MATTER...

11

...FOR A MAY MORNING.

12

BUT WHICH TWIN IS WHICH

THOU HAST, SEBASTIAN, DON GOOD FEATURE SHAME.

SEBASTIAN?

13

ARE ALL THE PEOPLE MAD?

IT LAST SANITY RETURNS, AND FOR SOME THERE IS A HAPPY ENDING.

GIVE ME THY HAND.

YOU ARE BETROTHED BOTH TO A MAID AND MAN.

■ Who's Who in *Twelfth Night*

Duke Orsino

Orsino, we are told, is 'a noble duke, in nature as in name' (1.2, line 23), but in the play we see little more than a love-sick melancholic who appears to enjoy dwelling on his own sad emotions. He does very little; rather, he simply reacts to other events. His one aim is to wed Olivia. In his three appearances in the first two acts he does nothing but talk of love, listen to sad music and send messengers to Olivia, never thinking of going himself. It is obvious in Act 2 that he feels an affectionate care for his servant Cesario. Then he disappears from the play while more active characters drive the plot forward. In Act 5 all the twists of the plot are put before him and, predictably, he reacts honourably. He is briefly furious with Olivia and Cesario, but tries to do justice to characters as different as Antonio and Malvolio and, when all becomes clear, happily accepts Viola as 'his fancy's queen' (5.1, line 378). The melancholy, the passionate love for Olivia, are forgotten: how deep-rooted were they in the first place?

Olivia

Olivia is a parallel character to Orsino. She shuts herself off in her palace and indulges a desperate grief, in the same way that he indulges a melancholy love. Just as he does, she changes instantly when the situation changes: when, in both cases, Viola/Cesario appears as a candidate for their love. Olivia is, however, different from Orsino in several ways and is a character to whom it is easier for audiences to relate. She is active, responds to many different people, shows wit and humour and pushes the plot forward. She can manage her household, exercises some control, at least, over such diverse types as Sir Toby and Malvolio, and enjoys Feste's clowning. Horrified by the bizarre behaviour of Malvolio (Act 3, Scene 4), she still shows some care for him. Above all, she pursues her hopeless love affair with some vigour, until, suddenly, it becomes hopeless no longer. Even in her self-indulgent mourning or her crazy love for Viola, she relates more to the real world and real people than Orsino does.

Viola/Cesario

In Shakespeare's comedies there is not one single central role, unlike the tragedies, such as *Hamlet* or *Macbeth*. However, it is very tempting to see Viola as the **protagonist** of *Twelfth Night*, as hero and heroine simultaneously. It is she who makes things happen, who disturbs the state of self-indulgent melancholy in Illyria and finds her way to a happy ending for both herself and the Illyrians. She is emotional, romantic and capable of strong attachments (to her brother, as well as to Orsino). From her first appearance (Act 1, Scene 2) she sees a link between herself and both Orsino and Olivia: incidentally, she makes sure that Orsino is a bachelor! As the youth Cesario, however, she is full of spirit, life and wit, confining her romantic impulses to such tales as that of her supposed sister: 2.4, lines 106–121. Here, as elsewhere, she teases her hearers with hints of her real person.

> **Viola** I am all the daughters of my father's house,
> And all the brothers too.

(2.4, lines 120–121)

We are given the impression that Viola is of a noble family, but not wealthy. Her independent spirit is typical of one who has to make her way in the world, equally at home with sea captains, jesters and aristocrats. Her mystery is maintained to the end when she never returns on stage to the Viola character and never replies directly to the Duke's proposal.

Note: It is often difficult to know what name to use for Viola. In this guide you are reminded of the truth from time to time by the use of 'Viola/Cesario'. In other cases whichever name seems appropriate has been used: there is bound to be some inconsistency.

Sebastian

Sebastian is a very important character in terms of the plot, but he is not developed individually. He is the male equivalent of Viola and shares all her characteristics of hope, courage and independence without having much chance to show them. He first appears briefly in Act 2, Scene 1, but becomes involved in the action only when the madness has reached its height. He, of course, will be the solution to the madness. Both Orsino and Olivia need a Viola/Cesario: Sebastian is the answer. You might note his confused willingness to respond to Olivia's proposals and his main difference from Cesario: his ability in combat!

Malvolio

Malvolio is the typical stern, puritanical steward, except that he is not driven by principle, but by conceit and self-love. Though he is ultimately treated most cruelly by Sir Toby, Feste and the others and his desire for revenge is very understandable, it is difficult to sympathise too much with him. His criticism of the drunken singing in Act 2, Scene 3, is again understandable, but one feels that he is enjoying the opportunity to treat his supposed superiors (the knights) as inferiors.

Malvolio My masters, are you mad?   *(2.3, line 81)*

His conceit and absurdity grow during the play until the humiliation of imprisonment subdues his self-importance. With Malvolio, it is important to remember that he is half-convinced that Olivia loves him even before Maria's clever letter exposes his vanity and folly.

Sir Toby Belch and Sir Andrew Aguecheek

Both of these knights devote their lives to the pursuit of pleasure. Sir Toby, it would appear, is the more successful in this pursuit. Though it is easy to see him as shallow and worthless, he probably does not see himself that way. His main delight is drunken revelry and his taste for practical jokes is limitless. Probably he has the audience's support in his ongoing skirmishing with Malvolio, but sympathy for him is reduced by his policy towards Sir Andrew. He deceives him without mercy and keeps him at Olivia's to gain access to his money. Sir Toby is an unlikely kinsman for Olivia, but at least he marries sensibly: to Maria. Sir Toby's humour owes more to energy than to subtlety, but he is a model of wit compared to Sir Andrew, whose humour is largely accidental, as are any comments of his that make sense. The appeal of Sir Andrew is as a simpleton and victim, but his appeal to the audience is strengthened because he readily admits his own failings. Unlike Malvolio, he never really believes that he has any chance of gaining the affections of Olivia.

Maria, Feste and Fabian

Olivia's servants more than match her uncle and his foolish friend in wit and intelligence, and it is interesting to see knights and servants operating as a group with very little indication of social differences. Maria is sharp, shrewd and witty, with the skill in composition and penmanship to deceive Malvolio and delight Sir Toby.

Feste, the jester, has perhaps the best understanding of the world of Illyria of any character. Not only does he supply plenty of witty fooling, but he shows Olivia the truth of her situation and is the only person besides Cesario to belong at both Orsino's court and Olivia's household. With his songs about love, death and growing up, he provides a wise and somewhat melancholy commentary on the play. Fabian is something of a mystery character. He was obviously introduced alongside Feste when Shakespeare realised that he was making too many demands on the Clown character. He is a servant, but intelligent and well-spoken: he explains events in polished **blank verse** in Act 5, Scene 1. What he shares with the entire household is a hearty dislike of Malvolio.

Sea Captains

Given the similarities between Viola and Sebastian, it is highly appropriate that their introductions to the play mirror each other: rescued from the sea, each talks with a Sea Captain, believes her/his beloved brother/sister dead and goes off to Orsino's court. The difference, of course, is that Antonio, Sebastian's sea captain, plays a significant part in the plot. Even considering the fulsome expressions of affection of the time, Antonio's devotion to Sebastian seems excessive. Perhaps it is another example of the appeal of the twins: people of both sexes love Viola very readily. The purpose of it in terms of plot is that Antonio's devotion, even to giving Sebastian his purse, both leads to further confusion (at the duel) and contributes to the solution of the mystery.

Act 1, Scenes 1–3

Plot synopsis

The play begins in the court of Orsino, Duke of Illyria. He is melancholy and lovesick for the Countess Olivia. She refuses even to see him or his messengers; instead she mourns her dead brother in solitude. The scene moves to the coast where Viola comes ashore after a shipwreck, fearing her brother may have died. She decides to disguise herself and remain in Illyria.

 Viola   I prithee (and I'll pay thee bounteously)
Conceal me what I am.

(1.2, lines 49–50)

The next scene brings another change of scene: to Olivia's house. There another would-be husband for Olivia appears, a very foolish knight, Sir Andrew Aguecheek. He is persuaded by Sir Toby Belch, Olivia's uncle, to stay and continue his hopeless courtship. The only advantage is to Sir Toby who has the use of Sir Andrew's money.

Text commentary

A world of contrasts

The three opening scenes provide considerable contrasts. Between two very different indoor scenes (one romantic, one comic) there is a dramatic outdoor scene. The characters, who all talk of love, have very different attitudes to it.

1 Orsino is melancholy in love

> *Orsino* If music be the food of love, play on,
> Give me excess of it, that, surfeiting,
> The appetite may sicken, and so die.
> That strain again! It had a dying fall;
> O, it came o'er my ear like the sweet sound
> That breathes upon a bank of violets,
> Stealing and giving odour. Enough, no more!
> 'Tis not so sweet now as it was before.
> O spirit of love, how quick and fresh are thou,
> That, notwithstanding thy capacity,
> Receiveth as the sea.

(1.1. lines 1–11)

Orsino claims that he wishes to cure his appetite for love. Music feeds love; too much ('excess') will cause loss of appetite, then the appetite will die. However, already in these first lines of the play, Shakespeare suggests Orsino's self-indulgent enjoyment of his melancholy. He asks to hear again his favourite tune ('strain') because it is sad ('had a dying fall') and stops it when he finds it is not so sweet as before.

You should note Shakespeare's use of **similes** to suggest Orsino's romantic melancholy. In lines 5–7 he extends the original comparison to give an **image** of sweet scents on a bank of violets. Compare this with the final couplet of the scene.

> Orsino   Away before me to sweet beds of flow'rs;
>   Love thoughts lie rich when canopied with bow'rs.
>
> *(lines 39–40)*

You will notice that Orsino uses his favourite adjective 'sweet' to describe the beds of flowers.

It is essential that you read the question very carefully and make sure that you answer all parts of it. Probably there will be a list of suggestions of what you might include in the essay. You do not have to plan your essay around these points, but they are very helpful in pointing you towards useful material.

Love dominates Orsino's world and, though in his opening description it sounds soft and gentle, it can be a fierce and destructive thing. Notice that, in another **simile**, it is compared to the mighty sea. See if you can work out the **pun** on 'hart'/'heart' (lines 16–24): a hart is a deer. You will again find the cruel and destructive side to love.

> Orsino   And my desires, like fell and cruel hounds,
>   E'er since pursue me.
>
> *(lines 21–22)*

In lines 23–31 Valentine tells how Olivia has vowed not to venture out of her house for seven years while she weeps for her dead brother. Orsino finds ground for optimism here (how devoted she will be when she falls in love!). What impression do her actions make on you? Can you compare her with Orsino?

2 Viola seeks employment

Viola   O that I served that lady,
And might not be delivered to the world,
Till I had made mine own occasion mellow,
What my state is.

I'll serve this duke.
Thou shalt present me as an eunuch to him;
It may be worth thy pains. For I can sing,
And speak to him in many sorts of music
That will allow me very worth his service.
What else may hap, to time I will commit;
Only shape thou thy silence to my wit.

(1.2 lines 38–41/52–58)

Viola's bold activity forms a contrast to the melancholy of Orsino and the shuttered mourning of Olivia. Note that Viola, too, has lost a brother – or so she thinks.

Viola   And what should I do in Illyria?
My brother he is in Elysium. *(i.e. in Heaven)*

(lines 2–3)

The Sea Captain is able to provide Viola with details of life in Illyria and she is drawn to both Orsino and Olivia. She seems able to take on the characteristics of the two nobles whom she admires. She talks of withdrawing from the world ('might not be delivered') with Olivia and charming the Duke with music.

In reading the question take note of key words that instruct you in what to do. If you are asked to compare, you must find similarities and differences between two or more things. If asked to explain, you must show why. Do not automatically tell the story, though you may need to include some narration if you are asked to 'give an account'.

What do we learn of Viola here? Her determination of character and her willingness to work (though she is clearly from a prosperous and probably noble family) are evident, but what facts about her background and reason for being in Illyria are given? You should notice her emphasis on concealment and secrecy. She does not want her true identity revealed until the time she chooses ('made mine own occasion mellow'). See how many references to concealment you can find in the last 25 lines of the scene.

3 Revellers and a hopeless suitor for the Countess Olivia

Toby   O knight, thou lack'st a cup of canary! When did I see thee so put down?

Andrew   Never in your life, I think, unless you see canary put me down. Methinks sometimes I have no more wit than a Christian or an ordinary man has. But I am a great eater of beef, and I believe that does harm to my wit.

Toby   No question.

Andrew   And I thought that, I'd forswear it. I'll ride home tomorrow, Sir Toby.

Toby   Pourquoi, my dear knight?

Andrew   What is 'pourquoi'? Do, or do not? I would I had bestowed that time in the tongues that I have in fencing, dancing and bear-baiting. O, had I but followed the arts!

(1.3 lines 76–90)

Of course, it is suitable that the first scene at Olivia's should not include her. She is shut away mourning her brother, though she appears two scenes later. It enables Shakespeare to present three different moods for the comedy in the first three scenes: romantic, active and clownish. However, we are able to get an impression of Olivia's character at second hand. Read Maria's warnings to Sir Toby in the first part of the scene before Sir Andrew enters.

> **Sir Toby** She'll none o' th' Count. She'll not match above
> her degree, neither in estate, years, nor wit; I have
> heard her swear't.

(lines 102–104)

Whether Sir Toby has heard her swear it is debatable, but he is right. She will have nothing to do with the Duke (Sir Andrew and Sir Toby are simply using 'Count' carelessly). Now think who she might turn to if she wants someone younger and poorer than herself.

The scene with Sir Andrew establishes him as a character of extreme stupidity. The puzzlement over 'pourquoi' is a good example: see what other cases of similar misunderstandings you can find elsewhere in the scene.

Sir Andrew and Sir Toby are knights; Maria is a fairly senior servant. You might like to compare their intelligence, wit and positions of trust with Olivia. There is certainly no huge social gulf! In particular, examine Sir Andrew's conversation with her, which contains sexual jokes that cast doubt on his manhood, notably when Andrew says, 'I would I might never draw sword again' (lines 59–60). Andrew appears as doltish and unmanly.

> **Maria**   My name is Mary, sir.
>
> **Andrew** Good Mistress Mary Accost.

(lines 50–51)

The scenes between Sir Toby and Sir Andrew are full of **slang** and usually contain several **puns**, as on 'put down', meaning defeat in conversation or fall over with drink. Later (line 114) Toby has fun with the meanings of 'caper' as 'dance' and 'spice'.

At the end of a test essay it is useful to sum up your opinions with a conclusion. However, it is more important to keep your main argument in view throughout, and simply repeating yourself in a lengthy concluding paragraph gains little credit.

Note the evidence of Sir Andrew's (and, by implication, Sir Toby's) way of life. 'Fencing, dancing and bear-baiting' have occupied his time, and dancing becomes the theme of the last part of the scene, Andrew exiting in a high-kicking dance. They should be happy as they think only of their own pleasure: do they appear as happy characters?

We are certain of one thing: Andrew's courtship of Olivia will come to nothing, but simply part him from his money. We do wonder how Olivia comes to have an uncle like Sir Toby.

Quiz

Can you trace the plot?

Three characters or sets of characters are presented in these first three scenes. Can you trace what happens when they meet?

a) In the next scene, Viola is at Orsino's court. Under what name?

b) What does Orsino feel about her? What does she feel about him? What task does he give her?

c) When Viola first goes to Olivia's house (Act 1, Scene 5), who delays her at the gate? How?

d) Who introduces whom to Olivia as 'a fair young man'?

e) What farcical scene does Sir Toby arrange between Viola and Sir Andrew in Act 3?

Can you find the image?

The main image of this play is of love. The Duke speaks of nothing else in the first scene; Viola and Olivia display love for brothers; Viola idealises both Duke and Countess and shows a readiness to love one or both. Which characters do the following references to love refer to?

a) Who is 'sick of self-love'?

b) Who sings to his mistress, 'your true-love's coming'?

c) Whose love and respect for a friend of the same sex is so great that he gives him all his money?

d) Who 'never told her love'?

e) Who is surprised to hear a lady he has never met declare her love for him?

Do you know these words?

Do you know the meaning of these words, all used in Act 1, Scenes 1–3?

a) 'distaff' (1.3, line 96)

b) 'accost' (1.3, line 45)

c) 'surfeiting' (1.1, line 2)

d) 'validity' (1.1, line 12)

e) 'practice' (1.2, line 12)

f) 'cloistress' (1.1, line 27)

g) 'canary' (1.3, line 76)

h) 'kickshawses' (1.3, line 108)

i) 'abjured' (1.2, line 37)

j) 'coranto' (1.3, line 120)

Sample question

What do we learn in the first three scenes of the play? Think about:

- *the characters and their relationships with each other;*
- *the plot, or story;*
- *the atmosphere or mood of the play.*

In your introduction, you might like to talk about the importance of the opening scene of any play. The writer needs to draw the reader or the audience into the story, give us some idea of what to expect from some of the characters, start us thinking about what might happen, how the different parts of the story might fit together. Writers do this by using a range of dramatic devices, which is what the rest of the essay is about.

Like all stories, there is a background, a history of things which have taken place before the play begins. We learn a lot of these very quickly. Orsino has been courting Olivia, without success, for some time. This immediately makes us wonder if he will ever be successful. Olivia has been mourning her dead father and brother. Viola has been shipwrecked and her brother lost at sea. We wonder if he has died. The fact that she is a stranger who has no friends or funds means that virtually anything could happen to her. Sir Toby is obviously exploiting Sir Andrew Aguecheek. How long can it continue?

Characters are carefully established, even in these first few pages. Viola is independent, resourceful and clever, capable of being decisive and determined. Find evidence in the things she says and does that supports these statements. When asking about Orsino, whom she has heard of but never met, she says 'He was a bachelor then'. Why do you think Shakespeare has included this hint so early in the play? Orsino seems to be deeply in love, but is he? How does Shakespeare suggest to the audience that even before they have met, Orsino and Viola are right for each other? Olivia does not appear until the last scene of the first act. Why do you think Shakespeare has arranged it this way?

Sir Toby Belch and Andrew Aguecheek provide a complete contrast to the other characters we meet, like Orsino, who are presented as noble and honourable characters. Find quotes in the play that sum up Sir Toby's character and which act as a contrast to Orsino's.

Although we are told about some serious and important events in these scenes, the mood is nevertheless, generally light-hearted. The fact that we begin with Orsino relaxing and listening to music sets the tone. Viola's plans to dress as a man suggest the comedy of mistaken identity that will follow. Sir Toby and Sir Andrew provide a more bawdy humour. Find lines in the scene that suggest particular moods and discuss them.

In your conclusion, talk about which of the characters you have met you feel most drawn to at this point in the play. Viola has lost everything, but is optimistic about the future. Orsino thinks love is more important than anything else in his life. Sir Toby has plenty of faults, but does he need sympathy?

Act 1, Scene 5

Plot synopsis

The first part of the scene is full of activity in Olivia's household. The Clown, Feste, and Maria joke together, then the entrance of Olivia shows that, despite her grief, she still derives enjoyment from Feste's fooling. Malvolio, the steward, disapproves.

Malvolio I marvel your ladyship takes delight in such a barren rascal.

(lines 78–79)

Maria, a drunken Sir Toby and Malvolio are all involved in announcing a visitor. Viola/Cesario has arrived with Orsino's messages of love. Surprisingly Olivia listens to the message and eventually dismisses all attendants. She still refuses Orsino's advances, but unveils herself and talks freely and animatedly. Olivia realises that she is falling in love with Cesario.

After Cesario has left, Olivia makes an excuse to send a ring after 'him' with Malvolio.

Text commentary

A House of Mourning?

In Act 1, Scene 3, we might have felt a little surprised at the cheery goings-on in a house dominated by Olivia's seven-year mourning. In this scene Olivia herself appears, but still Feste's clowning is popular and so is the handsome young messenger from the Duke.

1 The Clown and the Fool

Feste	Good madonna, give me leave to prove you a fool.
Olivia	Can you do it?
Feste	Dexteriously, good madonna.
Olivia	Make your proof.
Feste	I must catechize you for it, madonna. Good my mouse of virtue, answer me.
Olivia	Well, sir, for want of other idleness, I'll bide your proof.
Feste	Good madonna, why mourn'st thou?
Olivia	Good fool, for my brother's death.

Feste	I think his soul is in hell, madonna.
Olivia	I know his soul is in heaven, fool.
Feste	The more fool, madonna, to mourn for your brother's soul being in heaven. Take away the fool, gentlemen.

(lines 52–67)

You first need to recognise the meaning of the word 'fool'. It is an alternative word for 'jester' or 'clown', but it also has the present meaning. So, Feste can say to Olivia, 'Better a witty fool than a foolish wit' (lines 32–33), suggesting that a fool can be clever ('witty') and a supposedly wise man can be 'foolish'. Olivia, in sad mourning, orders the fool (clown) to be taken away and he retorts by saying she is the one who is a fool (in the modern sense).

What do you think about Olivia's behaviour here? Certainly she behaves frostily to Feste at first, but she is very soon intrigued and amused by his fooling, and she responds to the attacks of Malvolio (a foolish wit, perhaps) by defending satirical fools.

Olivia	There is no slander in an allowed fool.

(lines 87–88)

How deep is Olivia's grief? She is mourning her brother, certainly, but is she really inclined to cut herself off from the world for seven years? Let us look at how Feste amuses her. He plays games with words, saying 'dexteriously' instead of 'dexterously' and throwing in Latin phrases: 'Cucullus non facit monarchum' (lines 50–51) could be loosely translated as 'things are not always what they seem', a good motto for *Twelfth Night*.

In normal circumstances you should use formal correct English, avoiding slang and contractions (e.g. 'they've' for 'they have'). If you are writing in character, this will, of course, change, but clarity of expression is still the most important consideration.

The most obvious feature of Feste's **wit** is his use of a twisted form of logic. Anybody can understand why Olivia is mourning her brother, but his questioning of her makes it seem the height of folly – to be sorry that a loved one is enjoying the delights of heaven! You should also note the obvious affection which he feels for her. 'Madonna' simply means 'my lady', but you can find a more playful form of address which he uses.

Olivia's behaviour towards her household suggests a young lady very much in control, but not obsessed with her own dignity nor languishing in melancholy like Orsino. Her favour of Feste rather than Malvolio, her informal relationship with Maria and her ability to swap jests with her household are, perhaps, a surprise. Look, for instance, at her treatment of her drunken uncle. She wants him kept out of the way, but she is happy to put the Clown in charge of him and sends him on his way with a speech full of clownish wit.

| Olivia | Go thou and seek the coroner and let him sit o' my coz; for he's in the third degree of drink – he's drowned. Go look after him. |

(lines 128–130)

Notice how she finishes off a gag of Feste's, uses abbreviations like 'o'' for 'on', and the **slang** term 'coz' for 'cousin', used in Elizabethan times for other similar relationships, like uncle.

2 Viola pleads Orsino's love to Olivia

Viola   If I did love you in my master's flame,
With such a suff'ring, such a deadly life,
In your denial I would find no sense;
I would not understand it.

Olivia   Why, what would you?

Viola   Make me a willow cabin at your gate
And call upon my soul within the house;
Write loyal cantons of contemned love
And sing them loud even in the dead of night;
Hallo your name to the reverberate hills
And make the babbling gossip of the air
Cry out 'Olivia!'.

(lines 253–263)

Viola/Cesario begins well in her/his meeting with Olivia. She takes on the role of the brash and cheeky youth effectively, saying she does not wish to waste the speech on the wrong person and engaging in verbal by-play with Maria, the 'good swabber'. She adds mystery and allure to her earlier rudeness by hinting at secrets and romance.

> **Viola** What I am, and what I would, are as secret as maidenhead.
>
> *(lines 206–207)*

When she is left alone with Olivia, things become more intimate. They exchange quips about Orsino's heart; Olivia unveils herself; Viola (in her role as youth) alternates flattery and rudeness.

> **Viola** 'Tis beauty truly blent... *(line 228)*
>
> I see you what you are; you are too proud.
>
> *(line 239)*

He/she is making an impression on the supposedly remote Olivia, but it is not the impression that Viola wishes to make. Note that, at the end of the 'willow cabin' speech, Olivia is eager to know more about Cesario, but simply dismisses Orsino: 'I cannot love him' (line 270). Her instructions for future visits show how the situation is changing.

How does Viola make such an impact? She is active and eloquent, speaking in terms that suggest determination, sincerity and romance, using devices of style that sound natural in her forthright way of speaking. For instance, in line 254, she uses a vivid **oxymoron** ('deadly life') to describe Orsino's love. In the next speech she conjures up a telling **image** of besieging Olivia's house in a 'willow cabin' (willow is associated with distressed lovers), then claims Olivia's attention with richly **onomatopoeic** language: 'hallo', 'reverberate', 'gossip'.

Why she does it is more difficult to decide. She loves Orsino, so why put his case so strongly to another woman? Think about the following possibilities:

- she loves Orsino so unselfishly that she puts his wishes above hers;
- as one whose beloved does not think of her as a lover, she sympathises with his case;
- she is acting out her own sense of loss because Orsino does not notice her.

> **Viola** O, you should not rest
> Between the elements of air and earth
> But you should pity me.
>
> *(lines 263–265)*

Viola's mistake is to enter into the message so much that she almost acts out the part, with much use of 'I' and 'me'. Olivia confuses message and messenger.

3 Olivia in love

> **Olivia** 'What is your parentage?'
> 'Above my fortunes, yet my state is well.
> I am a gentleman.' I'll be sworn thou art.
> Thy tongue, thy face, thy limbs, actions and spirit
> Do give thee fivefold blazon. Not too fast: soft, soft,
> Unless the master was the man. How now?
> Even so quickly may one catch the plague?
> Methinks I feel this youth's perfections
> With an invisible and subtle stealth
> To creep in at mine eyes.
>
> *(lines 279–288)*

The irony is that Olivia, who attracts so many would-be husbands, falls instantly and completely in love with someone so unsuitable. Viola plays 'Cesario' very well, of course: remember that she imitates her twin brother.

Examiners know that you are writing against the clock and understand that there will be some errors of spelling, punctuation, etc. However, if you have time, it is always worthwhile to check your completed work thoroughly to reduce mistakes to a minimum.

Notice how Olivia is surprised by the speed of her reactions. The moment Cesario has gone, however, Olivia is replaying 'his' words. See how many words and phrases you can find in this speech that suggest either speed or surprise.

A further irony is Olivia's emphasis on Cesario being a 'gentleman'. The phrase 'five-fold blazon' refers to this. A blazon is the coat of arms a gentleman can display, and Cesario's claims are based on 'his' speech, face, limbs, actions and spirit. Of course, when Olivia insists that 'he' is a gentleman, she means that he is of good family and well bred, never thinking that 'he' lacks a more basic qualification.

This scene launches the **farcical** misunderstandings based around love and mistaken identity. Compare Olivia's last **soliloquies** with Viola's **aside** at the end of the previous scene.

  Viola   Whoe'er I woo, myself would be his wife.

(1.4, line 42)

Quiz

Can you trace the characters?

The confusion over the identities of Viola and Sebastian becomes a serious element in the plot in this scene and the following (Act 2, Scene 1). Viola's disguise as a male is seen here to be too effective; Sebastian's survival will spread further confusion. Can you identify the following incidents?

a) Who advises Cesario that 'his' choice of lover is 'too old' because, in love, the man should always be older than the woman?

b) What happens when Sir Toby and Fabian provoke a duel between Sir Andrew and Viola, thinking that she is a man?

c) What happens when, shortly afterwards, Sir Andrew and Sir Toby meet Sebastian and think that he is Cesario?

d) Who accuses Cesario, thinking him to be Sebastian, of denying him money?

e) What does Olivia do the first time she meets Sebastian?

Can you fill in the background?

The most important section of Act 1, Scene 5, is the interview between Olivia and Viola/Cesario, but there is also much background on Olivia's household. Who are these people?

a) Who is in danger of dismissal for staying away from Olivia's house?

b) Who is Olivia's confidential servant and attempts to prevent Cesario's private interview?

c) Who speaks 'nothing but madman'?

d) Who despises fools and jesters? What is Olivia's reaction to his words?

Do you know these words?

Do you know the meaning of these words, all used in Act 1, Scene 5?

a) 'swabber' (line 195)

b) 'points' (line 21)

c) 'misprision' (line 50)

d) 'zanies' (line 84)

e) 'blent' (line 228)

f) 'indifferent' (line 236)

g) 'blazon' (line 283)

h) 'inventoried' (line 234)

i) 'nonpareil' (line 243)

j) 'catechize' (line 57)

Sample question

What is your opinion of Olivia at this point in the play? You will need to think about:

- *her relationship with the other characters – how she treats them and how they treat her;*
- *the impression she gives us of her personality;*
- *her changing moods.*

In your introduction, you need to point out that this is the first appearance of Olivia. She is almost the last of the major characters that we meet. But we have already heard something about her from other characters.

When Olivia first enters, she orders the fool to be taken away. Why do you think she does this? Why doesn't the fool go? How does the fool feel about her and about the way she is living her life? Do you agree with him, and if so, why?

> Olivia   'O you are sick of self-love, Malvolio'

> *(line 85)*

Olivia does not seem to have a very high opinion of Malvolio. Why, then, does she employ him? The contrast between his outlook and Feste's is in direct contrast here, and the way Olivia deals with each one is important.

Although Olivia is clearly in charge, she doesn't seem to control Sir Toby very well. Does she give us the feeling that she is tolerant, that she does not care, or that she cannot make him act properly? Prove your point with a quotation.

Why does Olivia agree to see Viola? She seems to be attracted to her (in her disguise as Cesario) almost as soon as she meets her. How is their discussion different from those we have already heard in the scene? Look at lines such as, 'I will give out divers schedules of my beauty. It shall be inventoried, and every particle and utensil labelled to my will.'

Although Olivia is in mourning for her brother and father, she gives us the impression that she is bright and lively. She is independent, capable of making her own decisions, without being unduly influenced by others, yet she is prepared to listen to the views and advice of a wide range of people. She is prepared to make fun of her own beauty. Explain how each of these characteristics is important and how she compares with the other women in the play and with the men. Which seem most in control of their own lives?

In your conclusion, talk about how your opinion of Olivia has changed since the beginning of the scene, because of her relationship with Viola, Sir Toby and Malvolio. Many of the most important events of the play are linked to what happens here. How?

Act 2, Scene 5

..AND SOME HAVE GREATNESS THRUST UPON 'EM.

Plot synopsis

Sir Toby and Maria, with the participation of Sir Andrew and Fabian, play a cruel, and very amusing, trick on Malvolio. Annoyed by his open criticisms of their behaviour, they take advantage of his vanity and belief that Olivia would be willing to marry him.

> *Malvolio* To be Count Malvolio!
>
> *(line 32)*

Maria can imitate Olivia's handwriting and the trick consists of planting a letter, written by her but supposedly from Olivia, where Malvolio will find it. The letter drops obscure hints that Olivia loves him. Malvolio's behaviour is as vain, as gullible and as absurdly dignified as they could wish. Not only are the conspirators highly amused in this scene, but Malvolio is now set to obey the instructions in the letter with richly comic results.

Text commentary

The gulling of Malvolio

The scene is simply constructed. At start and finish there are sections of approximately 20 lines telling us what the conspirators have planned and what will happen next. Otherwise Malvolio holds centre stage with the hidden stage audience providing an amused and amusing commentary on his words and actions.

1 Malvolio is already half-deceived

Malvolio	Calling my officers about me, in my branched velvet gown, having come from a day-bed where I have left Olivia sleeping –
Toby	Fire and brimstone!
Fabian	O, peace, peace.
Malvolio	And then to have the humour of state, and – after a demure travel of regard, telling them I know my place, as I would they should do theirs – to ask for my kinsman Toby.
Toby	Bolts and shackles!
Fabian	O, peace, peace, peace, now, now.

> **Malvolio** Seven of my people with an obedient start make out for him. I frown the while, and perchance wind up my watch, or play with my – some rich jewel. Toby approaches; curtsies there to me.
>
> **Toby** Shall this fellow live?
>
> *(lines 44–59)*

In a Shakespearean play a **soliloquy** is usually to be taken as being true, as reflecting the actual thoughts of the speaker. This episode is, so far as Malvolio is concerned, a soliloquy: he does not know he is not alone. Leaving aside the dignity and self-control he shows in public, Malvolio is revealed as an absurdly vain and self-deceiving man.

You must note that, in over 50 lines before he finds the letter, Malvolio dreams without foundation of being married to Olivia. Note also that he does not dream of love, but of exerting authority over the likes of Sir Toby. When, later on, we feel some sympathy for Malvolio as the victim of Maria and Sir Toby's trick, remember the words that he spoke shortly after entering.

> **Malvolio** Maria once told me she did affect me.
>
> *(lines 21–22)*
>
> To be Count Malvolio!
>
> *(line 32)*

In this section about Sir Toby, Malvolio eventually plans to tell him off about his drunkenness, and you should note how he enjoys the thought of having power and status. For instance, he refers to 'Toby' and 'Olivia' by their first names, emphasises that Toby is his 'kinsman', imagines leaving Olivia in a day-bed, and so on. See what examples you can find of how he imagines people behaving towards him.

Malvolio sees himself as expensively dressed, wearing rich jewels, and there is an extra joke at his expense when he refers to 'play with my…' (line 57). This is generally thought to refer to his chain of office as a steward. He suddenly remembers he will no longer be a steward and changes the end of the sentence.

You should be able to make sure that you finish your essay in the test. However, if you run out of time before you have made all the points you want to, spend the last five minutes jotting down in note form what you intended to write. It is not ideal, but it is better than leaving them out altogether.

What impression are you given of Malvolio here? Look at the sort of language he uses as well as the opinions he expresses. What, on the other hand, do you think of Sir Toby? At every hint of Malvolio's pride he produces another colourful exclamation of fury: how does he react to references to himself in Malvolio's imaginary little scene? Sir Andrew's reaction to hearing ill about himself is quite different.

Malvolio	'Besides, you waste the treasure of your time with a foolish knight.'
Andrew	That's me, I warrant you.

(lines 72–74)

By the time Malvolio reaches the letter, we know the sort of reaction to expect from him and also from the watchers.

2 Malvolio solves the problem

Malvolio	'I may command where I adore, But silence like a Lucrece knife With bloodless stroke my heart doth gore. M.O.A.I. doth sway my life.'
Fabian	A fustian riddle.
Toby	Excellent wench, say I.
Malvolio	'M.O.A.I. doth sway my life.' Nay, but first let me see, let me see, let me see.
Fabian	What dish o' poison has she dressed him!
Toby	And with what wing the staniel checks at it!

Malvolio 'I may command where I adore.' Why, she may command me. I serve her, she is my lady. Why, this is evident to any formal capacity. There is no obstruction in this. And the end – what should that alphabetical position portend? If I could make that resemble something in me. Softly – 'M.O.A.I.'

(lines 100–115)

The comedy of this scene comes from various sources. One is the behaviour of the onlookers. They enjoy Malvolio's gullible remarks and praise Maria ('excellent wench') for the 'dish o' poison' which so totally deceives him. Most of the lines are spoken (often in pairs) by Sir Toby and Fabian. Sir Toby, predictably, makes mocking or threatening comments about Malvolio: sometimes mocking *and* threatening. Do Fabian's comments differ in any way from Sir Toby's? You might have expected Feste to be present, rather than Fabian. Can you think of any reason why Shakespeare might have omitted the Clown? You should consider:

- where Feste is in surrounding scenes;
- the impact of scenes like Feste-as-Sir-Topaz;
- what part Feste might have played in this scene.

 Malvolio 'M'. Malvolio. 'M' – why, that begins my name.

(line 119)

Another source of humour is Malvolio's twisting of the evidence to suit his wishes. The rhymes and the letter are cleverly written to give him little real evidence, but enough to work on. In the 'I may command ...' rhyme, the first line does suggest Malvolio as a possibility, but the references to the story of Lucrece do not relate to him and the letters provide a test of his ingenuity. He himself says he wishes to 'make that resemble' his name, and so he does.

 Malvolio ... to crush this a little, it would bow to me, for every one of these letters are in my name.

(lines 132–133)

Maria is suitably subtle. Malvolio is given a hint, but, if it had read 'M.A.I.O.', he would have seemed less foolish and less funny.

Before an examination, make sure that you revise the whole text. You will be concentrating particularly on one scene, but you will also need to make reference to other parts of the play.

In the text there are few references to actions, but this scene is potentially full of visual humour which you can deduce from the lines. Consider how you would produce it, to bring out this visual humour. How, for instance, would Malvolio's appearance add to the comedy of his foolish and self-deluding words? What would his gestures and expressions reveal about his feelings? Above all, what comedy could be derived from the watchers and their positions and actions on stage? How would you build humour from the fact that they might be discovered and the joke spoiled?

3 The letter

Malvolio 'If this fall into thy hand, revolve. In my stars I am above thee, but be not afraid of greatness. Some are born great, some achieve greatness, and some have greatness thrust upon 'em. Thy fates open their hands, let thy blood and spirit embrace them, and to inure thyself to what thou art like to be, cast thy humble slough, and appear fresh. Be opposite with a kinsman, surly with servants. Let thy tongue tang arguments of state; put thyself into the trick of singularity. She thus advises thee that sighs for thee. Remember who commended thy yellow stockings, and wished to see thee cross-gartered. I say remember, go to, thou art made if thou desir'st to be so; if not, let me see thee a steward still, the fellow of servants, and not worthy to touch Fortune's fingers. Farewell. She that would alter services with thee, The Fortunate Unhappy.'

(lines 134–150)

The letter is certain to convince Malvolio: 'let me see thee a steward still' is the most obvious hint yet. The joy of the comedy is now largely in anticipation. We gradually learn what Malvolio is likely to do next. He will fall out with Sir Toby ('be opposite with a kinsman'); he will become eccentric ('the trick of singularity') and talk pompously about politics; he will appear before Olivia in yellow stockings, cross-gartered. In the postscript (lines 163–167) come instructions to smile.

 Malvolio I will smile, I will do everything that thou wilt have me.

(lines 167–168)

The praise Maria receives is well deserved. She explains to her companions and to us at the end of the scene (lines 187–194) that she has chosen fashions and manners that Olivia hates so that they will see 'the fruits of the sport' when Olivia and Malvolio next meet.

The letter is also written with great skill and cunning. There is a sense of elegance and dignity which matches Malvolio's view of the world and himself. The famous sentence about greatness is beautifully balanced and instantly memorable. Hints of rhymes ('tongue tang') add to the polish of the style. Even the signature ('The Fortunate Unhappy') is an **oxymoron**. See how many unusual or pompous words or phrases you can find: 'revolve' and 'Thy fates open their hands' are two examples.

 In the examination you will have a copy of the scene in front of you to remind you of any quotation you need. However, it is worth learning key quotations. Examinations are against the clock and it helps to know what quotations you are looking for and where they are to be found. You may also wish to quote from another part of the play.

Malvolio's complete acceptance of the terms of the letter and his exalted and self-important joy ('Jove, I thank thee' – line 167) add to the comedy. Ask yourself how far Malvolio is justified in believing the letter. There are some strong clues, but you should also be able to find plenty of self-delusion when he meditates on Olivia's previous reactions to him.

At the end of the scene we expect the even more absurd follow–up scene immediately: 'If you will see it, follow me' (lines 193–194). It is, in fact, delayed until Act 3, Scene 4. In the meantime there is further **farce** with Sir Andrew, and a count-down on Malvolio's progress from Maria. The result is that the audience is built up to a frenzy of comic anticipation.

Quiz

Can you trace the character?

This is a very funny scene which leads to another very funny scene, but it also has a serious effect on how other characters perceive Malvolio. Can you follow his character through the play?

a) What does Olivia decide to do with Malvolio after his appearance before her (Act 3, Scene 4)?

b) How does Malvolio misunderstand her intentions at that time?

c) What punishment does Sir Toby arrange for him?

d) What part does Feste play in this punishment?

e) Why does Olivia decide to release him?

f) How successful is Malvolio in regaining his former status?

Can you identify the insult?

The watchers make many insulting remarks about Malvolio and he makes as many about them. Can you find the following insults and criticisms and identify who is speaking about whom?

a) 'a rare turkeycock'

b) 'the niggardly rascally sheep-biter'

c) 'a foolish knight'

d) 'You must amend your drunkenness'

e) 'a contemplative idiot'

Do you know these words?

Do you know the meaning of these words, all used in Act 2, Scene 5?

a) 'fustian' (line 104)

b) 'consonancy' (line 122)

c) 'staniel' (line 109)

d) 'jets' (line 29)

e) 'branched' (line 44)

f) 'Tartar' (line 195)

g) 'aqua vitae' (line 186)

h) 'gin' (line 79)

i) 'probation' (line 123)

j) 'inure' (line 138

Sample question

This is one of the scenes in the play in which humour is very important. How does Shakespeare make it funny? Before you start writing, think about

- *the characters of those involved;*
- *the use of stage devices, such as the positions of the characters;*
- *how the scene fits in with the way love is portrayed in the play.*

In your introduction make some general points about the humour in the play. Not all of the play is funny, but there is a general feeling that the characters ultimately enjoy life, that any problems they face are fairly minor and can be overcome. Shakespeare uses the same kind of humorous devices throughout the play – wit, or wordplay, mistaken identity and slapstick are all used to highlight Malvolio's conceit, Sir Andrew's foolishness and Sir Toby's drunkenness.

Each of the characters who appears in the scene contributes to the comedy, though it is the interaction between them that is most important. Explain how a feeling of excitement and mischief is built up as Sir Toby and the others enter and hide themselves, like children expecting a treat. Each time Sir Toby's anger increases and the others try to prevent him attacking Malvolio, his situation seems more ridiculous. Malvolio is already thinking about Olivia as he enters. As he interprets the letter he has found as a compliment to himself, look at how his pride swells.

The fact that he is the only one who can't see how wrong he is makes him seem ridiculous too. Show how Shakespeare builds up the contrast between how Malvolio sees himself and how the others view him. Pick out what you consider to be the most important lines and explain them. Similarly, look at how Sir Andrew's lines fit into the scene. Point out some of the contrasts in the language. How, for example is Fabian's observation that 'Contemplation makes a rare turkeycock out of him; how he jets under his advanced plumes', (2.5, lines 28–29) different from Malvolio's own 'calling my officers about me, in my branched velvet gown' (2.5, lines 44–45)?

This is a very visual scene and depends for its success on what we see as well as what we hear. Explain why it is important that Sir Toby and the others are hidden from Malvolio but can be seen by the audience. Whereabouts on stage would you position Malvolio? Why? You could increase the comic effects by thinking about the use of props: as Sir Toby gets more agitated, there might be things that he could almost knock over.

Malvolio is led to think that he might marry Olivia, but is there any evidence in this scene that he does not really love her? Does Orsino love Olivia? Why is Olivia attracted to Viola? Why does it take Sir Toby most of the play to realise that he and Maria are an excellent match? These are all questions that lead us to look at what love really means in the play. Some characters seem well matched from the beginning, though they may not realise it themselves. Much of the play is concerned with working out the problems in order to get to the right solutions.

In your conclusion, pick out what you consider to be the funniest moments in the scene and explain what attracts you to them.

Act 3, Scene 1

Plot synopsis

Viola/Cesario returns to Olivia's to try to persuade her to look favourably on Orsino. The scene is divided in two, with a brief interlude with Sir Toby and Sir Andrew in the middle. In the first part Cesario swaps witticisms with Feste, the Clown, and lives up to his reputation as a smart and clever youth. Sir Andrew, in fact, is overcome with the elegance of Cesario's words to Olivia.

> *Andrew* That youth's a rare courtier; 'rain odours' – well.
>
> *(lines 84–85)*

The second half of the scene is another meeting of Olivia and Cesario alone. No real progress is made, but Olivia becomes more open and more passionate. Viola drops occasional hints throughout the scene as to her real identity, but only for the audience's understanding. The scene ends with another request from Olivia for the youth to visit, with the excuse that maybe she will change her mind about Orsino.

Text commentary

Viola – 'a rare courtier'

This scene shows Viola's wit impressively engaged with various members of Olivia's household, notably the Countess herself. Let us see how Viola copes with various situations: the final one very difficult and potentially disastrous.

1 Wit and foolery

Viola   Art not thou the Lady Olivia's fool?

Feste   No, indeed, sir, the Lady Olivia has no folly, she will keep no fool, sir, till she be married, and fools are as like husbands as pilchards are to herrings – the husband's the bigger. I am indeed not her fool, but her corrupter of words.

Viola   I saw thee late at the Count Orsino's.

Feste   Foolery, sir, does walk about the orb like the sun, it shines everywhere. I would be sorry, sir, but the fool should be as oft with your master as with my mistress. I think I saw your wisdom there.

Viola   Nay, an thou pass upon me, I'll no more with thee. Hold, there's expenses for you.

Feste   Now Jove in his next commodity of hair send thee a beard.

| *Viola* | By my troth I'll tell thee, I am almost sick for one, |
| | though I would not have it grow on my chin. |

(lines 30–46)

Viola and Feste exchange jests from the start of the scene. Feste's **puns** on living by the church are based on two meanings of 'live by': 'make a living out of' and 'live near'. Viola is happy to act as his straight man, but also caps his jokes from time to time. Feste is an inventive beggar, rewarded for his comic ingenuity by Viola. The joke in lines 50–51 refers to the story of Pandarus, who brought together the lovers Troilus and Cressida. In the same way Feste would like to bring together two coins – to breed, he says.

Feste comments on the folly of husbands with the pilchards/herring simile (lines 32–33). Is this comment justified? Are husbands shown to be foolish? Perhaps all those who seek Olivia's hand are. The male/female confusion of the play is also expressed in a joke. Feste praises Cesario and hopes he will soon have a beard: in other words, will grow to adulthood. Viola turns it round to her wish to gain Orsino's love. Do you think that Feste understands the joke? Is he the only one to see through her disguise?

When you plan your essay, make a clear decision about what each paragraph is going to be about. If at all possible, make it clear what the subject or topic of the paragraph is in the first sentence, often called a 'topic sentence'.

Another regular theme of the play is the conflict between folly and wit. **Wit** can often seem the more foolish. Here Feste uses a disarmingly modest phrase about his occupation (a 'corrupter of words'), but speaks up for the importance of foolery shining everywhere. Viola agrees in her **soliloquy** after Feste's departure.

| *Viola* | This fellow is wise enough to play the fool, |
| | And to do that well craves a kind of wit. |

(lines 59–60)

2 Wit and foolishness

Andrew Dieu vous garde, monsieur.

Viola Et vous aussi, votre serviteur.

Andrew I hope, sir, you are, and I am yours.

Toby Will you encounter the house? My niece is desirous you should enter if your trade be to her.

Viola I am bound to your niece, sir; I mean she is the list of my voyage.

(lines 70–76)

The brief scene with the two knights shows Viola's wit in a different setting. With Feste there is a spontaneous double-act, though not quite as equals as Feste, the professional, begs money from Viola. Here Sir Toby and Sir Andrew attempt to establish their superiority over this youth who is making Sir Andrew's wooing even more desperately difficult. They fail totally in this.

Sir Andrew attempts French; Cesario responds confidently; Sir Andrew reverts to English. Sir Toby attempts fanciful language ('encounter the house'). Cesario squashes him with a plain-sounding answer containing a neat **pun**: 'bound to' means 'obliged to' and 'heading for'. Sir Toby's next attempt at affected style ('taste your legs' – line 77) comes to nothing when Cesario forces him to put it in plain English and answers 'with gait and entrance' (line 81). See if you can work out the pun on the word 'gait'. Eventually all Sir Andrew can do is plan to imitate Cesario.

 Andrew 'Odours', 'pregnant', and 'vouchsafed' – I'll get 'em all three all ready.

(lines 88–89)

Sir Andrew will later be persuaded to attempt revenge on this witty and courtly youth – to hilarious (and, ultimately, very painful) effect.

44

3 Love confessed and denied

Olivia   I prithee tell me what thou think'st of me.

Viola   That you do think you are not what you are.

Olivia   If I think so, I think the same of you.

Viola   Then think you right, I am not what I am.

Olivia   I would you were as I would have you be.

Viola   Would it be better, madam, than I am?
    I wish it might, for now I am your fool.

Olivia   *(aside)* O what a deal of scorn looks beautiful
    In the contempt and anger of his lip!
    A murd'rous guilt shows not itself more soon
    Than love that would seem hid. Love's night is noon.

(to Viola) Cesario, by the roses of the spring,
    By maidhood, honour, truth and everything,
    I love thee so that maugre all thy pride,
    Nor wit nor reason can my passion hide.

(lines 136–150)

The final challenge to Viola's **wit** in this scene comes in the much more serious form of her need to withstand Olivia's advances. She says, 'I pity you' to Olivia in line 121, but Olivia sees scorn, contempt and anger in her look (lines 143–144). Which do you think is the more accurate view of Viola's feelings about Olivia?

Olivia throughout this scene attempts to keep some self-control, but her passion keeps bursting through her attempts at dignity. 'Enchantment' is a word that shows her hopelessness in the face of her passion. She turns Viola's 'I pity you' into a sign of hope: 'That's a degree to love' (line 121). She then regains a hold on her dignity, saying that it is time for Cesario to go, and managing a generous farewell.

Olivia Be not afraid, good youth, I will not have you.

(line 129)

In a moment, however, she is calling on 'him' to stay and asking what 'he' thinks of her. *Twelfth Night*, like many of Shakespeare's plays, often deals with the difference between appearance and reality. Viola's 'I am not what I am' makes obvious sense: she is not Cesario, she is not even male. In what sense is Olivia 'not what you are'? Not in love with a young man, as she thinks? Not really mourning her brother? Not the sort of person she pretends to be?

You will have long enough in your tests to prepare the essay properly. Use the reading time sensibly by deciding what are the main points you need for your essay, making a list of them and planning in what order you are going to deal with them.

Olivia's **aside** (lines 143–146) shows how powerless she is in the grip of her emotion. Love is no more capable of remaining hidden than a guilty secret. The **metaphor**, 'Love's night is noon', means that, even when it wishes to remain as dark as night, love will always shine out and reveal itself.

The result is an open declaration of love, made more formal by the use of rhyming **couplets** and by swearing an oath by maidenhead, honour and truth. How is Viola to respond? She replies in similar style, swearing an oath and using **couplets**. Read lines 155–158 and work out how she can reassure Olivia about the affections, while concealing the truth about her feelings and her true nature.

Viola I have one heart, one bosom, and one truth,
And that no woman has.

(lines 156–157)

The themes of **wit** and folly run throughout this scene. Olivia's passion cannot be controlled by 'wit' (cleverness/intelligence) or reason (line 150), and the word 'wit' is particularly associated with Viola.

| | Olivia | And yet when wit and youth is come to harvest |
| | | Your wife is like to reap a proper man. |

(lines 130–131)

Viola also complains of being Olivia's 'fool' (line 142). Think back to what Feste said about Olivia, her fool and her potential husband. How does the Fool, Feste, compare in wit and reason with his mistress, the wise Countess?

Quiz

Can you find the Clown?

Feste claims that 'foolery... does walk the orb like the sun'. He is described as 'Olivia's jester', but he is the only character besides Viola who regularly moves between the households. Can you find these events involving Feste?

a) He contributes to Orsino's love of music. Can you name the sad song he sings in Act 2, Scene 4, and find a line which is particularly suitable to Orsino's love-melancholy?

b) What famous comic scene does he not take part in, perhaps surprisingly? Where might he have been at that time?

c) Whom is Feste 'sent for' by Olivia? Whom does he find (Act 4, Scene 1)? What does he go to report to Olivia?

d) In the character of Sir Topaz, of what does he try to convince Malvolio?

e) Feste sings the last words of the play. Can you sum up the themes of his last song in a few words?

Is she telling the truth?

Viola is by nature honest and truthful, but is in a position where she is forced to deceive. How truthful do you think the following remarks are?

a) 'I am almost sick for one (a beard), though I would not have it grow on *my* chin.' (lines 45–46)

b) 'Your servant's servant is your servant, madam.' (line 100)

c) 'Then think you right, I am not what I am.' (line 139)

d) 'I have one heart, one bosom, and one truth,
   And that no woman has.' (lines 156–157)

Do you know these words?

Do you know the meaning of these words, all used in Act 3, Scene 1?

a) 'maugre' (line 149)

b) 'cypress' (line 119)

c) 'tabor' (stage direction at the start of the scene)

d) 'welkin' (line 57)

e) 'baited' (line 117)

f) 'upbraids' (line 128)

g) 'gait' (line 81)

h) 'commodity' (line 43)

i) 'loath' (line 23)

j) 'feigning' (line 97)

Sample question

Comment on the different sides of Viola's personality that we see in this scene. You will need to think about:

- *her conversation with Feste;*
- *her meeting with Olivia;*
- *how her disguise as a man affects our view of her.*

In your introduction you should mention that at least some of the success of this play depends on Viola's ability to convince the other characters that she is a man, while at the same time reminding the audience that she is not. This scene, in which Olivia falls even more deeply in love with the character that Viola has adopted, is a good example of the kind of dual awareness the audience must have while watching the play. Because of this at least some of Viola's remarks can be read in two different ways, as a man and as a woman. At the same time, we need to feel some sense of sympathy with her if we are going to identify with her. The meetings she has in this scene help to show different sides of her character: comic and serious, male and female.

At the end of her conversation with Feste, Viola recognises that Feste is 'Wise enough to be a fool', and that to take part in this kind of wordplay takes a special kind of intelligence. Remember that wit, or the ability to play with words was, to an Elizabethan audience, a way of showing how clever you are. Pick out some examples of their witty conversation such as 'She will keep no fool, sir, till she be married' (line 32) and 'her name's a word and to daily with that word might make my sister wanton'.

Viola shows an honourable and honest side to her character in her conversation with Olivia. She has been sent to tell Olivia how much Orsino loves her – and she does try, even though she doesn't want to, having already fallen in love with him herself. The more Viola tries, the more Olivia wants to talk about her instead. Viola shows us a different side of herself to that which Olivia sees. Lines like 'I pity you' (line 121) for example, sound hard and cruel to Olivia, but how do we interpret it?

Viola goes through several mood changes as the scene progresses. She seems most relaxed when talking with Feste. With his ability to twist what he says, he seems to know that things are not always what they seem on the surface, but at the same time is happy to keep the conversation on a light-hearted level. It never becomes personal and so her disguise is never threatened. When she talks to Sir Toby she is less sure of herself and remains very polite. With Olivia she is desperate to put her off her line of questioning. What different methods does she use to achieve this? Olivia says, 'O what a deal of scorn looks beautiful In the contempt and anger of his lip' (3.1, lines 143–144). What does this tell us about what Viola is feeling and what she is trying to do?

In your conclusion, talk about why this scene is important. Viola's loyalty to Orsino shows that she deserves to win him. Her awkwardness with Sir Toby and Sir Andrew points the way to the challenge later in the play. Her cleverness helps the audience to accept her as a deserving heroine, someone we want to win in the end. Why is the fact that she is not completely in control of what is happening important?

Act 3, Scene 4

Plot synopsis

Malvolio appears, looking ridiculous and behaving absurdly, before Olivia who is astonished and concerned. The humour continues after her exit when Sir Toby, Maria and Fabian treat him as a madman, but he still believes that he is well in favour with Olivia who wishes him to be rude to kinsmen and servants.

> **Malvolio**   Go hang yourselves all. You are idle shallow
> things, I am not of your element.
>
> *(lines 118–119)*

The focus of comedy changes when Sir Andrew brings the challenge he has written to Cesario. It is, of course, nonsense, so Sir Toby plans instead to deliver the challenge by word of mouth and terrify both Cesario and Sir Andrew with reports of the other's prowess. After a brief episode between Olivia and Cesario, preparations for the duel go ahead, with much unwillingness on both sides.

> **Viola**   I am one that had rather go with Sir Priest than
> Sir Knight.
>
> *(lines 261–262)*

When they are finally brought together Antonio intervenes, thinking Viola/Cesario is Sebastian. He accuses Viola of ingratitude when he is arrested for earlier enmity to Orsino and (s)he is unable to return his money. She, on the other hand, is delighted to hear him name 'Sebastian'. The scene ends with Sir Toby planning another attack by Sir Andrew on the apparently cowardly Cesario.

Text commentary

Matter for a May morning

This extremely long scene consists of a series of absurd set-pieces, arranged by Sir Toby and the others, with two short serious sections: the last visit of Viola to Olivia and the arrest of Antonio. Overall, this scene is full of what Olivia calls 'midsummer madness'.

1 Malvolio attempts to achieve greatness

> **Olivia**   Why, how dost thou, man? What is the matter
> with thee?

Malvolio	Not black in my mind, though yellow in my legs. It did come to his hands, and commands shall be executed. I think we do know the sweet roman hand.
Olivia	Wilt thou go to bed, Malvolio?
Malvolio	'To bed? Ay, sweetheart, and I'll come to thee.'
Olivia	God comfort thee. Why dost thou smile so, and kiss thy hand so oft?
Maria	How do you, Malvolio?
Malvolio	At your request? Yes, nightingales answer daws.

(lines 23–34)

 Malvolio's appearance is particularly well prepared for, not only in the letter scene, but also in the build-up where Maria tells Sir Toby and Fabian (Act 3, Scene 2) and then Olivia (the beginning of this scene) of Malvolio's behaviour. As a result, there needs to be no explanation and the humour flows instantly. Verbally much of the scene with Olivia consists of quotations from the letter and Olivia's astonished reaction.

Much of the humour is visual, deriving from Malvolio's clothes and manner. When he says, 'Not black in my mind, though yellow in my legs' (line 24–25), it not only draws attention to his appearance, but shows how proud he is of it, twisting a query about his health into an opportunity to show off his legs. When Olivia mentions bed (to rest, to recover) he launches into a bawdy ballad and makes his intentions very clear.

Malvolio says, 'commands shall be executed' (lines 25–26) and he puts all the instructions in the letter into practice. See what examples you can find (between lines 14 and 120) of Malvolio obeying the instructions about how to behave to kinsmen and servants.

Follow through Malvolio's behaviour from the short scene with Olivia to his soliloquy and the scene with Sir Toby, Maria and Fabian. The **soliloquy** (lines 62–80) is a masterpiece of self-deception. Everything is twisted to suit the words of the letter.

Malvolio No worse man than Sir Toby to look to me. This concurs directly with the letter.

(lines 62–64)

Timing your test essays is important. As the test proceeds, check your progress against the clock in the room. Make sure that you are giving yourself enough time to finish, but also check that you are not progressing too rapidly. If you finish very early, you have not included enough detail, so, if you realise this is going to happen, develop your arguments at greater length and add more references and quotations. Finishing 5–10 minutes early is a good idea, leaving time to check your work.

Why does Malvolio, thinking of the letter, believe that Olivia is sending Sir Toby to him? Has she, in fact, chosen Sir Toby specifically? A similar delusion comes with the word 'fellow' that Olivia uses. Originally it meant 'companion' (in that sense, 'equal'), but it came to be applied to inferiors. You can work out which meaning Olivia intends and which Malvolio understands.

Malvolio … nothing that can be can come between me and the full prospect of my hopes.

(lines 78–79)

Malvolio must have spent the scene in a dream of self-congratulation to believe that 'no scruple of a scruple' lies between him and marriage to Olivia. Notice the frequent thanks to Jove: what other scene does this remind you of?

Sir Toby, Maria and Fabian enter, full of talk of madness and possession by the devil. See how many references to devils and fiends you can find. This poor crazed thing must be treated jovially, so Sir Toby calls him 'my bawcock', 'chuck' and 'biddy' (lines 108–111), all terms of endearment originally referring to chickens! Malvolio's indignant responses are taken to suggest that he is in league with the devil.

Malvolio My prayers, minx?

Maria No, I warrant you, he will not hear of godliness.

(lines 116–117)

The mocking of Malvolio has already extended further than the appearance before Olivia. Now Sir Toby plans the next stage: he will be bound in a darkened room. Are things starting to go too far?

2 The Challenge

Sir Toby (reads) Youth, whatsoever thou art, thou art but a scurvy fellow.'

Fabian Good, and valiant.

Sir Toby 'Wonder not, nor admire in thy mind why I do call thee so, for I will show you no reason for't.'

Fabian A good note, that keeps you from the blow of the law.

Sir Toby 'Thou com'st to the Lady Olivia, and in my sight she uses thee kindly; but thou liest in thy throat, that is not the matter I challenge thee for.'

(lines 143–152)

This introductory phase to the duel scene is more sharply written and contains more happy nonsense than the longer section after Viola has parted from Olivia who, as always, asks 'him' to 'come again tomorrow'. In the section beginning line 211, there is much visual humour of the quaking Sir Andrew and Viola, while Fabian and Sir Toby pile fairly conventional praise on the ferocity of the opponent. Note, by the way, that Sir Toby again cheats his 'friend', as he has done throughout.

Sir Toby (aside) Marry, I'll ride your horse as well as I ride you.

(line 271)

The challenge itself, which he proudly claims has 'vinegar and pepper in't' (line 139) is a typical product of the brain of Sir Andrew Aguecheek. Though never delivered to Cesario, it is read out by Sir Toby, no doubt in a suitably mock-heroic tone, to the accompaniment of **ironic** comments from Fabian.

The opening line shows a complete collapse of logic. The refusal to give a reason (line 147) is no doubt meant to sound bold, but just sounds silly. Having given the reason for the challenge (Olivia using Cesario kindly), Sir Andrew accuses Cesario of lying (line 151) when he (Andrew) is the only person to have mentioned it. See if you can find further failures of logic, phrases that do not make sense, in lines 160–164.

> Quotations are useful in an examination essay, but should be kept fairly short. You should quote a line or two, set out on the page as in the text, or fit a few words into your own sentence, identifying the quotation with speech-marks.

The whole duel scene is part of the growing sense of unreality and lunacy that builds up in Acts 3 and 4, to be carried to its climax with such scenes as Sebastian being whisked off to his betrothal to an unknown woman and Feste imitating Sir Topaz. Nothing is as it seems. Sir Toby and Fabian speaks in lies; Sir Andrew pretends to be a valiant fighter; Viola pretends to be a man. By the time the duel is ready to start, neither of the duellists has any wish to take part.

> *Andrew* Pray God he keep his oath.
>
> *Viola* *(aside to Andrew)* I do assure you 'tis against my will.
>
> *(lines 299–300)*

At this point reality breaks in, in the form of Antonio, who can and will fight and who has a history that will lead to real imprisonment, not the version that Sir Toby and Feste impose on Malvolio.

3 News of Sebastian

> *Antonio* Let me speak a little. This youth that you see here
> I snatched one half out of the jaws of death,
> Relieved him with such sanctity of love,
> And to his image, which methought did promise
> Most venerable worth, did I devotion.
>
> *First Officer* What's that to us? The time goes by, away.

Antonio	But O, how vile an idol proves this god!
	Thou hast, Sebastian, done good feature shame.
	In nature there's no blemish but the mind.
	None can be called deformed but the unkind.

(lines 350–359)

Antonio has previously been involved in sea battles against Orsino: hence his arrest. His speeches here introduce a different note into the play from the 'midsummer madness' preceding them. His words on love are very significant. In speaking of Sebastian he constantly uses religion as a **metaphor**. He refers to 'sanctity' and 'image' as though Sebastian is someone to be worshipped. See how many other words referring to religion you can find. It is always difficult to place Antonio's feelings for Sebastian precisely. Perhaps it is best to see them as part of a pattern of excessive emotion in love.

Look, too, at what Antonio says about beauty and goodness. In this play many characters judge others by appearances. Antonio stresses the importance of virtue. The greatest fault is to be 'unkind', which has the present meaning but also the sense of 'unnatural'.

His words about Sebastian point the way to the solution to the confusions of the plot. Viola, aware that she imitates her brother exactly, realises that he must be alive, and points out the importance of this in a series of rhyming **couplets**.

Viola	He named Sebastian. I my brother know
	Yet living in my glass.

(lines 370–371)

O if it prove,

Tempests are kind, and salt waves fresh in love!

(lines 374–375)

Before Sebastian's presence solves the confusion, it will first increase it. At this stage in the play each comic scene ends by anticipating further chaos. This time Sir Andrew is persuaded into following Cesario to beat him. There is certain to be a mistake of identity!

Quiz

Can you trace the character?

Sir Toby has tended to make things happen to suit himself up to this stage in the play. With the co-operation of others he has played tricks, sometimes cruel ones, on Malvolio, Cesario and Sir Andrew.

From now on he is more on the defensive. Can you trace his progress?

a) How does his attempt to continue the duel between Sir Andrew and Cesario go wrong? Mention two misfortunes that befall Sir Toby.

b) Half-way through the Sir Topaz scene (Act 4, Scene 2) he changes his mind about the plot against Malvolio. How and why?

c) His success in cheating Sir Andrew will end with Olivia's betrothal to Sebastian. What signs are there in Act 5, Scene 1 of his changed relationship with Sir Andrew?

d) What has Sir Toby to fear at the end of the play?

Can you tell who is mad?

As the play moves further into chaos and disorder, references to madness become more frequent. Can you find the following (in Act 3, Scene 4) and identify who is speaking about what?

a) 'Why, we shall make him mad indeed.'

b) 'The man grows mad, away with him.'

c) 'Why, this is very midsummer madness.'

d) 'I am as mad as he,
If sad and merry madness equal be.'

e) '... for sure the man is tainted in's wits.'

Do you know these words?

Do you know the meaning of these words, all used in Act 3, Scene 4?

a) 'cockatrices' (line 189)

b) 'daws' (line 34)

c) 'virago' (line 265)

d) 'yare' (line 217)

e) 'miscarry' (line 60)

f) 'the Sophy' (line 269)

g) 'present' (line 336)

h) 'arbitrement' (line 252)

i) 'bum-baily' (line 171)

j) 'tainted' (line 13)

Sample question

If you were directing this scene, how would you bring out its most important qualities? You will need to think about:

- *how Malvolio speaks and acts;*
- *Sir Andrew's challenge and Viola's reaction;*
- *the different moods that are created at different points in the scene.*

You may occasionally be asked for a response to the play which asks you to be more creative than is possible in an essay, but you need to remember that the basic aim of the question is the same. The person marking the piece wants to see how well you have understood the play. Some people forget this. But to gain maximum marks, you need to keep in mind the question and what you have learned while studying the play. Here you are asked to think about the dramatic qualities of the text, so you need to consider the fact that this is a play you are supposed to watch, not just read.

In your introduction outlining 'the most important qualities' in the scene will help to show that you are focusing on this right from the start, and will provide points for you to develop later in the essay. There is a lot of comedy, and some more serious moments. There is a great deal of misunderstanding, some of which is deliberately planned and some of which is not. There is much about love, some of which is imagined and some real. Most of all, there is the difference between what the individual characters know and what the audience knows.

Up until now, we have seen Malvolio as serious, sober and superior. Now he becomes ridiculous. How are you going to bring this out? Think about his tone of voice as he speaks to each character and how he might change this. Pick out some of his key lines. Explain why they are important and how they would be spoken. 'To bed!', for example, should provoke a strong audience reaction. Describe the way he should smile and think about other gestures he might use – a bow to Olivia, turning his back on Toby, a flick of his handkerchief – and explain why each would be effective.

The misunderstandings continue when Sir Andrew challenges Viola. Again the audience is in on the joke: we know that Andrew is a coward and Viola is a woman. In your stage directions, pick out key points where you can remind the audience of these facts, without giving the information to the others. Think about the way Sir Toby reads the challenge, keeping a serious face for Sir Andrew while letting the audience see how ridiculous it is. Even whereabouts on stage each character stands might be important.

Shakespeare deliberately increases the comic effect by making each of the characters react in completely different ways to the things that happen. Olivia is horrified by Malvolio's declaration, but then makes herself seem ridiculous in pursuing Viola. How are you going to show this? Viola seems very much in control of the situation when talking to Olivia, but is out of her depth when challenged. Sir Andrew seems keen enough to deliver his challenge, until he hears what a fighter Viola is supposed to be and then he changes his mind. All of these differences are brought out in the dialogue in the play, but you can emphasise them by thinking clearly about what the characters do on stage.

In your conclusion, remind the reader that the language of the scene is important, but so is the way the lines are delivered and the visual effects on stage. A theatrical experience is a combination of these effects.

Quiz

ANSWERS

ACT 1, SCENES 1–3

Can you trace the plot?

a) Cesario

b) He likes her and tells her all his secrets. She is in love with him. He sends her to woo Olivia on his behalf.

c) Sir Toby with drunken talk; Malvolio with excuses like Olivia being asleep.

d) Maria; Cesario (Viola)

e) A duel which never quite takes place.

Can you find the image?

a) Malvolio according to Olivia (1.5, line 85)

b) Feste: 'O mistress mine' (2.3, lines 37–38)

c) Antonio's for Sebastian (Act 3, Scene 3)

d) 'His' father's daughter, (i.e. Viola) as s/he tells Orsino (2.4, line 110)

e) Sebastian when he first meets Olivia (Act 4, Scene 1)

Do you know these words?

a) a pole used in spinning flax

b) approach, go alongside

c) having too much

d) value

e) method

f) nun

g) sweet wine

h) little tricks (from French 'quelque chose')

i) given up

j) a dance (many other dances are named here, like 'cinquepace' and 'galliard')

Act 1, Scene 5

Can you trace the characters?

a) Orsino (2.4, lines 28–30)

b) They are reluctantly about to start when Antonio breaks up the duel, thinking that Viola is Sebastian (Act 3, Scene 4).

c) He beats them severely and they end up in disgrace with Olivia (Act 4, Scene 1).

d) Antonio (Act 3, Scene 4)

e) She invites him to her house (4.1, line 52). Shortly afterwards they become betrothed.

Can you fill in the background?

a) Feste (lines 15–17)

b) Maria (tries to send Cesario away – line 194 – and is sent away herself – lines 209–210)

c) Sir Toby (lines 101–102)

d) Malvolio (lines 78–84. She tells him off for being 'sick of self-love' (line 85).

Do you know these words?

a) sailor who mops down the decks

b) laces for stockings/the modern meaning of 'matters'

c) misunderstanding or wrongful arrest

d) straightmen or stooges

e) blended

f) moderately

g) coat of arms

h) listed (as on an inventory)

i) unequalled

j) to question

Can you trace the character?

a) Place him in the care of Sir Toby (lines 58–59).

b) He thinks that Toby is brought before him so that he can be 'opposite with a kinsman', as in Olivia's letter (lines 66–67).

c) Imprisonment, bound, in a darkened room (line 130).

d) He torments Malvolio in the role of Sir Topaz, the priest (Act 4, Scene 2).

e) She receives his letter insisting that he is not mad (5.1, line 306).

f) He receives Olivia's promise (5.1, lines 344–346) that he will be able to try his own case, but whether he will ever regain his dignity and status is unclear.

Can you identify the insult?

a) Fabian about Malvolio (line 28)

b) Sir Toby about Malvolio (lines 4–5)

c) Malvolio about Sir Andrew (line 73)

d) Malvolio about Sir Toby (line 69)

e) Maria about Malvolio (line 17)

Do you know these words?

a) imitation silk (therefore language that sounds good, but means little)

b) consistency

c) kestrel

d) struts

e) decorated with patterns of branches

f) Hell

g) brandy or whiskey

h) trap

i) proof or test

j) make used to

ACT 3, SCENE 1

Can you find the Clown?

a) 'Come away, come away, death'. There are various suitable lines; perhaps the best choice would be: 'I am slain by a fair cruel maid' (line 53).

b) The scene where Malvolio reads the letter (Act 2, Scene 5). Feste is in the scenes on either side of it: at Orsino's court (Act 2, Scene 4), and meeting Viola at Olivia's house (Act 3, Scene 1). Maybe Shakespeare imagined him as still returning from court.

c) He claims he has been sent for Sebastian (4.1, lines 1–2). Obviously it was Cesario he was sent for, though he finds Sebastian. He reports to Olivia that Sir Toby and Sir Andrew have attacked 'Cesario' (in reality Sebastian).

d) That he (Malvolio) is mad (Act 4, Scene 2).

e) Growing up, the development of self-knowledge, the sadness of the world.

Is she telling the truth?

a) True, even perhaps to the extent of suggesting her secret.

b) Logically true, but deceiving, as 'servant' here also means devoted lover; today we would say 'slave'. In that sense Orsino is Olivia's servant; Viola is Orsino's servant; but Viola definitely is not Olivia's servant.

c) True, though in the terms of this conversation Olivia is expected to think it means something different (social class, perhaps).

d) Again strictly true, but very deceptive. It implies that 'he' is not in love. There is also another slight hint of the truth in 'no woman ... save I alone.'

Do you know these words?

a) despite

b) a veil (also the tree found in graveyards)

c) small drum

d) heaven (used as an impressive word for 'world')

e) tormented (as in bear-baiting)

f) reproves, tells off

g) movement, going

h) consignment

i) unwilling

j) pretence

Act 3, Scene 4

Can you trace the character?

a) 'Cesario' turns out to be Sebastian. Sir Toby is attacked by Sebastian; in Act 5, Scene 1 he is still limping. He falls into disgrace with Olivia (4.1, line 49).

b) He wants to end it as quickly as possible because Olivia is already so offended with him (4.2, lines 66–71).

c) He no longer has to encourage Sir Andrew and be friendly with him. In lines 199–200 he says what he really thinks of him: 'Will *you* help – an ass-head, and a coxcomb, and a knave; a thin-faced knave, a gull?'

d) Olivia has promised Malvolio he will be 'plaintiff and judge/Of thine own cause' (lines 345–346). Sir Toby may fear Malvolio's revenge.

Can you tell who is mad?

a) Fabian describing what will happen to Malvolio in prison (line 128).

b) First Officer arresting Antonio (line 362).

c) Olivia describing the behaviour of Malvolio before her (line 53).

d) Olivia comparing herself and Malvolio (lines 14–15).

e) Maria describing Malvolio before his entrance (line 13).

Do you know these words?

a) mythical creatures which could kill with a look (also called 'basilisks')

b) jackdaws

c) a fierce female warrior (interestingly applied to Viola/Cesario)

d) ready

e) suffer harm

f) the Shah of Persia

g) ready money

h) decision (in this case decided by death – 'mortal')

i) a bailiff who pursues debtors

j) diseased